ANCIENT EGYPT

Contents

Introduction

This is a map of Egypt. Egypt is a country in North Africa. The River Nile which flows through it is one of the longest rivers in the world.

The Ancient Egyptians are famous for their civilisation which lasted for several thousand years.

▲ This is a wall painting of an Ancient Egyptian king called Amenophis I.

LOOKING AT EVIDENCE

In Egypt today we can see many wonderful things that were made by people who lived long ago.

▼ This pyramid and sphinx at Giza were built by the Ancient Egyptians.

More than four and a half thousand years ago, when Britain and Northern Europe were still in the New Stone Age, life in Egypt was very different.

In Egypt

- They built with stone and mud bricks. Some buildings, like the pyramids, can still be seen today.

- Copper was melted down to make tools and weapons.

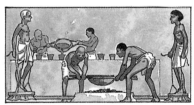

- They made pottery on a wheel and baked it until it was hard.

- They invented a form of writing and recorded their history.

In Britain and Northern Europe

- They used mainly wood and rushes for building.

- Tools and weapons were made from stone.

- They made poor pottery by hand and it was baked at low temperatures.

- They painted pictures but did not use writing.

India

d Sea

Arabian Sea

Ancient Egyptians liked to wear ellery. These necklaces would e belonged to a wealthy person, they are made of gold and jewels.

The River Nile

The White Nile, together with the Blue Nile which joins it in the south, has a total length of about 1,913 miles. The Blue Nile rises in the highlands of Ethiopia.

Egypt is very hot and very dry. There is not enough rain in Egypt to help crops to grow, so the River Nile is very important to the Egyptians.

▲ The River Nile today. Look at the dark soil on the banks of the river.

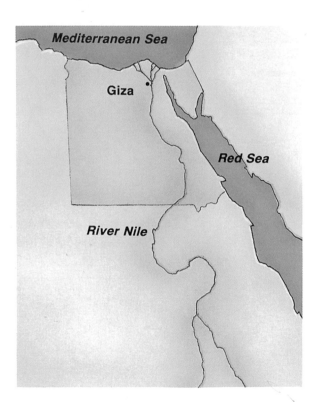

◄ Map showing the River Nile.

In the winter the water in the River Nile is at its lowest level.

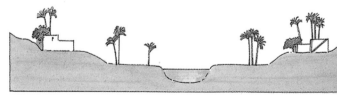

In the summer the Nile bursts its banks and floods the farm land on either side.

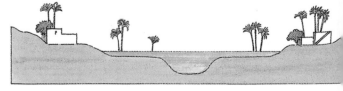

Every year it rains hard in the distant mountains to the south. In the summer, water comes rushing down the Nile into Egypt. The river bursts its banks and floods the farm land on either side.

▶ The shaduf was used in Ancient Egypt to help raise water from one level to another, and is still used by some farmers in Egypt today.

er the floods the farm land
a rich black mud. This land
ood for growing crops.

The Egyptian people have always used irrigation. In this way they can make the best use of the flood waters. The Ancient Egyptians dug ditches which ran through their fields. They built reservoirs to store the water. Men and women called conscripts were made to help with this work.

King Tutankhamen

In 1922 a man called Howard Carter discovered an Ancient Egyptian tomb. He carefully made a hole in one corner of the door. Then he lit a candle and put it inside. As his eyes got used to the light, he saw strange animals, statues and gold everywhere. His companions asked him, "Can you see anything?" All Carter could manage to say was, "Yes, wonderful things". The picture below shows what Carter saw.

Howard Carter was the first person to step inside that tomb for more than 3,000 years. Yet it looked as if it had only been sealed yesterday. On the wall he noticed fingerprints left by the Ancient Egyptian painter as he finished his work and left the tomb.

▲ The site of Tutankhamen's tomb.

▼ Inside Tutankhamen's tomb.

▲ **Howard Carter and an archaeologist studying Tutankhamen's coffin.**

◄ **King Tutankhamen in his palace.**

Carter discovered that this was the tomb of a young Egyptian king called Tutankhamen. The king's body had been buried in another room behind a wall of solid gold.

From early times robbers have broken into the tombs of Ancient Egyptians and taken away gold and silver goods, jewellery and other precious objects. Only a small part of Tutankhamen's tomb had been robbed. The thieves had not broken into the main room where the king's body lay. Tutankhamen was not a very important ruler, but his tomb is important because it was found almost intact.

Archaeologists

Archaeologists work like detectives to find evidence for what happened in the past. Here are some of the things that archaeologists can tell us about Tutankhamen even though he was buried so long ago and cannot tell us himself!

LOOKING AT EVIDENCE

By studying the finds and paintings in Tutankhamen's tomb – they can tell us how the Egyptians used to live.

▲ This is Tutankhamen's death mask. It is decorated with the head of a bird and a snake. The bird represents southern Egypt and the snake northern Egypt. From this archaeologists can tell us that Tutankhamen ruled the whole of Egypt.

◄ This is Tutankhamen's golden throne. By studying objects like this they can tell us that the Ancient Egyptians were skilled craftspeople.

In Egypt today we can see many wonderful things that were made by people who lived long ago. These objects have been dug up by archaeologists. The ancient Egyptians also made huge buildings like the pyramids which are still standing today. But they did not have lorries or machines to help them.

▼ By studying the Egyptian paintings and writing (called hieroglyphics) in Tutankhamen's tomb – they can tell us who the king was and when he lived.

This picture shows just how many coffins Tutankhamen was buried in.

The pharaohs

The kings and queens of Ancient Egypt were called pharaohs. The Egyptians believed that the pharaoh was the son of a god. Everything he said had to be obeyed.

The pharaohs also led the army. They conquered foreign lands near to their own. People from other countries had to bring gold and other gifts to the pharaoh. Large ships carried metals, wood, wine and olive oil from the port of Byblos in the north. These goods were then taken along the Nile by boat. Goods came from the south overland by donkey. Camels were not used at this time. Journeys by land were long and dangerous.

The pharaohs used the money they were given to build fine tombs and temples.

▲ Statue of Ramses II.

◀ This wall painting shows people bringing gifts as tribute to the pharaoh.

One pharaoh called Ramses the Second fought against people from the north called the Hittites. The battle of Kadesh was the most famous in Egypt's history. The result was a 'draw', but both sides claimed that they had won!

Some other pharaohs

Amenophis the Third

One pharaoh was called Amenophis the Third. One of Amenophis the Third's wives was called Tiye. Queen Tiye came from Nubia which is south of Egypt. She was well-educated and had a library of books on poetry, history, science and religion.

▼ **Statue of Amenophis III.**

Queen Hatshepsut

The pharaohs were usually men. Queen Hatshepsut's father was a pharaoh and so was her husband. When her husband died she made herself ruler. Queen Hatshepsut ordered many fine temples to be built.

Queen Hatshepsut had some huge obelisks cut from granite. One of these can still be seen at Karnak in Egypt. Obelisks were 30 metres long and weighed 390 tons each. Huge boats were built specially to carry them down the river from the quarry many miles away.

▲ **An obelisk in Karnak, Egypt.**

◄ The temple of Hatshepsut.

Hatshepsut sent some Egyptians on a trading expedition to a place called Punt. They took with them necklaces and daggers, and they brought back wood, ivory, animal skins and <u>incense</u> trees to plant in Egypt. The expedition is recorded in pictures on the walls of Queen Hatshepsut's temple at Deir el-Bahri.

Farmers and food

Farmers

In Ancient Egypt there were three seasons. In the first season (summer) the Nile flooded the farm land. In the second season the land was no longer flooded and the farmers ploughed, sowed seeds and dug new irrigation canals. The third season was the harvest.

▶ **A wall painting showing a man and woman ploughing and sowing seeds.**

Ploughs were made of wood. They were pulled by oxen and used to turn over the soil ready for the seed to be sown.

Irrigation canal

Hoes were used for breaking up heavy soil and for digging.

Boundary stone

How Ancient Egyptians made bread

1 Grain is knocked out of the emmer using a pestle and mortar.

2 A stone is rolled over the grain to make a fine flour.

3 Flour and water are mixed to make dough.

4 The dough is baked in a cone-shaped oven.

The Egyptians grew barley and a kind of wheat called <u>emmer</u>. The grain was made into flour and kneaded with water into a <u>dough</u> to make bread. Both rich and poor people ate bread and drank beer. They also ate fruits such as dates and figs. Those who could afford it would have meat, fish and wine. Meat from ducks and geese (and fish caught in the Nile) was pickled and dried in the sun.

Building a pyramid

These pyramids were built about 4,500 years ago. Some of the pharaohs were buried in pyramids when they died. The largest is the Great Pyramid of Cheops.

In these pictures you can see how the Egyptians may have built the Great Pyramid. It would have taken many years to build.

▲ Priests work out the direction of North.

► The site of the pyramid is marked out.

▼ The stone is quarried.

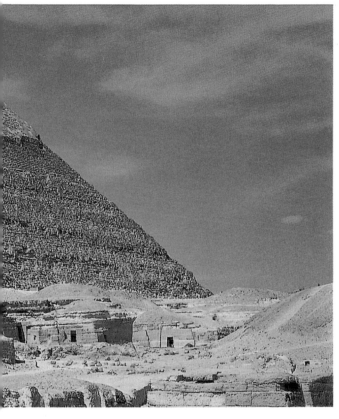

The Ancient Egyptians did not have cranes or pulleys to help them lift heavy stones. They had to find a way of lifting the pieces of stone to the right height. For this they used ramps made of earth. First they made sloping paths. Then they dragged blocks of stone along them on sledges. All their buildings were made using ramps, rollers and levers.

They only had tools made of bronze or copper. These metals are not as hard as the steel which is used for tools today.

◀ The pyramid of Chephren at Giza.

▼ The stone is dragged on a sledge up a ramp.

▼ Levers and rockers are used to slide each stone into place.

People at work

Builders and craftspeople

The people who built the pyramids, temples and tombs were of two sorts. The <u>conscripts</u> did much of the heavy work in large gangs. In later times men and women captured from other countries were sometimes used as slaves. The craftspeople, like the stone carvers and painters, were skilled. They decorated the insides of tombs with pictures and <u>hieroglyphics</u>.

Villages have been found where craftspeople lived. Here young people used to work in gangs doing odd jobs. They hoped that one day they too would become skilled craftspeople themselves. Then they would be able to work for the pharaoh.

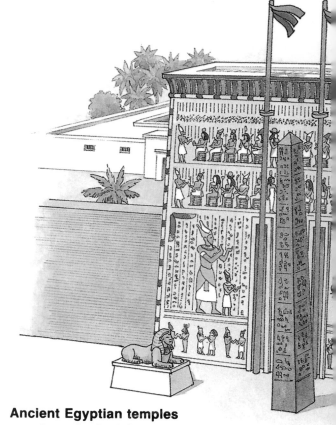

Ancient Egyptian temples may have looked like this.

LOOKING AT EVIDENCE

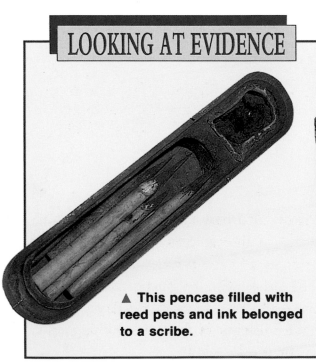

▲ **This pencase filled with reed pens and ink belonged to a scribe.**

▲ **Wall painting showing metal-workers and jewellers at work.**

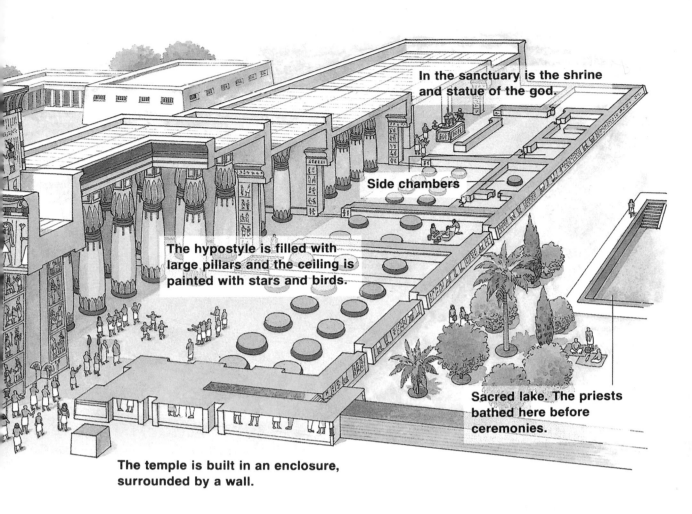

In the sanctuary is the shrine and statue of the god.

Side chambers

The hypostyle is filled with large pillars and the ceiling is painted with stars and birds.

Sacred lake. The priests bathed here before ceremonies.

The temple is built in an enclosure, surrounded by a wall.

Scribes

Scribes were very important in Ancient Egypt because they could read and write. They worked in the temples and also worked for the pharaoh. They were able to keep detailed written records of everything the pharaoh did. They also worked on building sites, and wrote down how much stone, mud bricks and sand was needed.

Only boys were allowed to become scribes. They went to schools run by priests. Here they learned to write with a reed pen. They had to copy out long pieces of writing. They also learned arithmetic.

POINTS OF VIEW

In Ancient Egypt only boys were allowed to train as scribes. Do you think this was fair?

Priests

Priests also had a very important job to do in the temples. Each temple was built as a home for a god or goddess. The priests had to make offerings to the god or goddess every day. They gave presents of food or clothing and burnt frankincense.

Life in an Egyptian house

▲ A painted wooden toy horse with wheels.

◄ A doll made of wood and clay with a painted face and beads to look like hair.

Children stayed with their mother until they were about four years old. Like children today they had many toys to play with.

The children of the pharaohs and other important people spent their time inside the palace with the women. When they were four years old they started lessons. They had their own teachers. In these rich families girls as well as boys were given lessons.

We know about life in rich people's houses from paintings and from remains that archaeologists have dug up. Houses were often built of mud bricks, which were painted white to keep them cool. Around each house were buildings where the servants lived and worked, kitchens and store-rooms. Gardens were very important to the Egyptians. They were filled with flowers and often had pools.

Clothing

Egyptian men and women wore simple clothing woven from plain linen cloth, which is light and cool to wear. The cloth was wrapped around the body. Sometimes it had pleats, but patterned and coloured cloth were not common. Wearing jewellery was very popular and many Egyptians shaved their heads and wore wigs.

▲ **An Egyptian wig.**

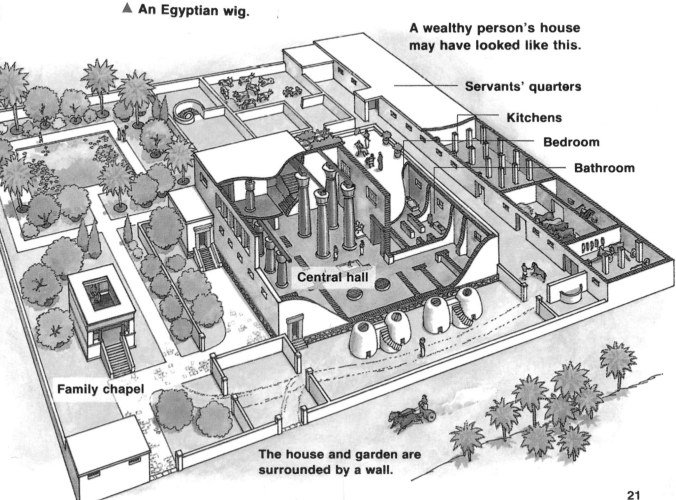

A wealthy person's house may have looked like this.

Servants' quarters

Kitchens

Bedroom

Bathroom

Central hall

Family chapel

The house and garden are surrounded by a wall.

People at play

This picture (right) is from the tomb of Nebamun. He was a scribe. It shows Nebamun with his wife and daughter. When he was alive Nebamun enjoyed hunting in his spare time. He is shown catching wild birds. In one hand he is holding a throwing stick. In the other he is holding three herons to help him attract other birds.

▼ **Wealthy women playing senet.**

▲ This is the board and some of the pieces used for playing senet. Each player usually had seven pieces. These were kept in the drawers.

Most people in Ancient Egypt, including Queen Nefertari, enjoyed playing a board game called <u>senet</u>. This popular game was played by two people, like draughts.

Another thing that rich people enjoyed was banquets. The wall painting below shows a banquet. Look for the women playing musical instruments and the dancers at the bottom of the painting.

Gods and goddesses

The Egyptians had many gods and goddesses. They believed the gods and goddesses looked after them by day. People prayed to the gods and goddesses in the hope that they would be rewarded. Sometimes they wrote their prayers down on stone. They also made carvings of ears hoping their god would listen!

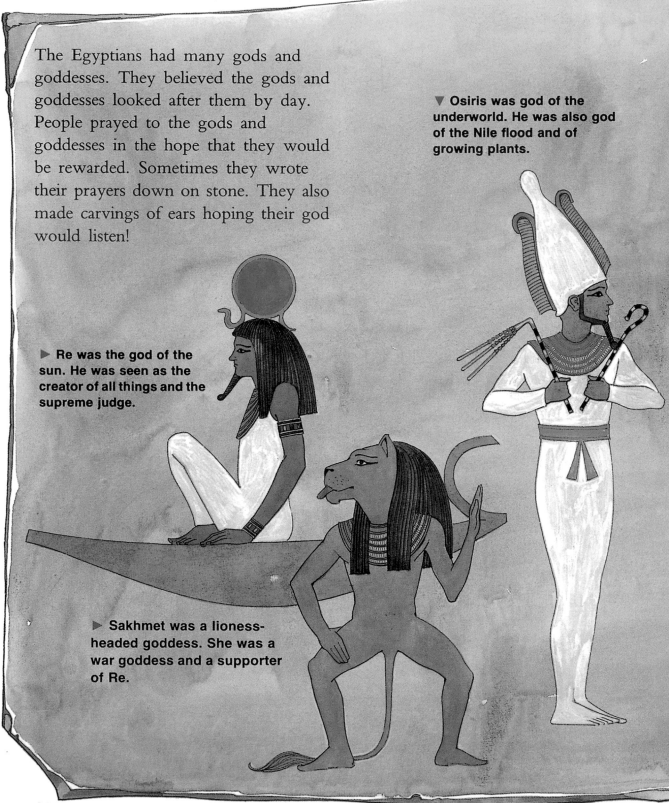

▼ Osiris was god of the underworld. He was also god of the Nile flood and of growing plants.

► Re was the god of the sun. He was seen as the creator of all things and the supreme judge.

► Sakhmet was a lioness-headed goddess. She was a war goddess and a supporter of Re.

◄ Isis was a mother goddess. She protected the coffins of people who died and was a mourner at their funerals.

► Bastet was the cat goddess, nd daughter of Re, the sun od. She was a kind and enerous protector.

◄ This bronze statue of a cat was sacred to the goddess Bastet.

Festivals were held for the gods and goddesses at different times of the year. These were holidays when people could enjoy themselves. The people gave thanks to the gods and goddesses when things went well for them. Here is an Egyptian thank you to the god of the River Nile:

> Praise to you Nile, who flows out of the earth and comes to feed Egypt... you who waters the meadows whom Re has made to feed all the cattle.

Most important to the Egyptians was their local god or goddess. This would be the god or goddess who had a temple nearby.

Egyptian writing

Papyrus

The papyrus plant once grew well in the Nile delta. Papyrus was used for making a kind of paper. This was done by beating strips of pith from the plant into flat sheets. The scribes wrote in red or black ink using their reed pens on the papyrus.

Many Egyptians were buried with a book made of papyrus. This was called *The Book of the Dead*. The Egyptians believed that this book helped the person to have a new life after death. Many writings on papyrus have been found. There are religious books, poetry, stories and magical spells.

1 Workers gather papyrus.

2 The outer case of the papyrus is peeled off. The inner core is cut into strips.

3 Papyrus strips are laid horizontally and vertically to make a page.

4 Cloth is put on the papyrus. It is beaten with a mallet.

5 The papyrus paper is rubbed smooth with a stone. Scribes write on papyrus using reed pens.

Hieroglyphics

This picture (left) with hieroglyphic writing is from the tomb of Hunefer the scribe. Look for Hunefer's tomb. Two women are shown: one of them is Hunefer's wife. They are mourning the dead man. You can also see four priests in the picture. One is wearing the head of a jackal. This made him look like Anubis, the god of funerals.

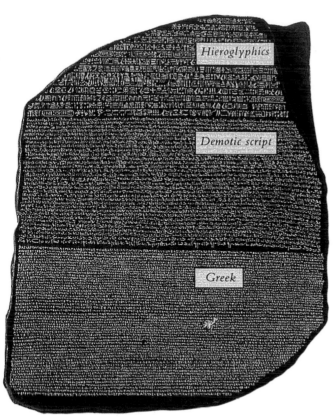

Hieroglyphics

Demotic script

Greek

▲ The Rosetta Stone is covered with two types of Egyptian writing and Greek.

Rosetta stone

For a long time no one knew what Egyptian hieroglyphics meant. One day an 11 year old French boy called Jean Francois Champollion was shown some hieroglyphics. He made up his mind that he would work out what they meant. Some years later Champollion found out the answer. He worked out what the hieroglyphics meant using the Rosetta stone. (This is now in the British Museum in London.) It is a black stone slab covered with writing. It has two kinds of Egyptian writing and also says the same thing in Greek. The names of rulers like Ptolemy, Alexander and Cleopatra are written in Greek. Champollion was also able to pick out these names in the Egyptian writing. This helped him work out what some of the hieroglyphics meant.

▲ Jean Francois Champollion understood Greek. He compared the Greek writing with the Egyptian hieroglyphics.

▼ After 14 years Jean Francois Champollion broke the code. He worked out the symbols for the letters 'p', 'l' and 'o'.

P T O L M I S

K L E O P A T R A

Ancient Egypt lives on

Life for the Ancient Egyptians went on in much the same way for hundreds of years. Even in later times when Egypt was ruled by the Greeks and the Romans, many things carried on as before. Visitors from other countries, like the Greek Herodotus, came to admire the pyramids. In modern times, archaeologists have dug up hundreds of papyri from the sands of Egypt. These have been translated and tell us how people lived. They still mummified their dead and worshipped gods like Isis.

Inventions

The Egyptians learned how to make glass by melting sand and adding chemicals. Later on, in Roman times, glass makers travelled all over the ancient world making their bowls and bottles. The Romans copied other ideas from Egypt.

▲ **Temple at Abu Simbel.**

Calendars

Ancient Egyptian priests studied the movement of the stars and the sun in the sky. Coffin lids have been found with calendars drawn on them. These calendars were made to help the dead know what day it was. The Egyptians worked out that there were 365 days (and a little bit extra) in one year.

Mathematics

The Egyptians knew a lot about mathematics. The flooding of the river was so important to them, that they used a Nilometer to record carefully each year how far the water level rose. They used geometry to measure and to work out the size of each farmer's land after the flood had washed away the boundary marks.

We know from a papyrus that the Egyptians knew about triangles with right angles long before the Greek mathematician Pythagoras. This helped them to build the pyramids.

Egypt today

Today many visitors go to Egypt to see the sites of Ancient Egypt.

The temples of Abu Simbel were built by Ramses the Second. When a modern dam was going to be built, people thought that the ancient temples would be flooded. So the temples were first taken to pieces. They were then carried to a safer place and put together again like a huge jigsaw puzzle. This is just one of the wonders of Ancient Egypt that you can still see today.

Glossary

These words are underlined in this book.

Archaeologists
People who have been trained to excavate (dig up) historical sites. They study objects they find and tell us what life in the past may have been like.

Conscripts
People who are made to do something. The pharaohs made many conscripts build the pyramids.

Dough
A mixture of flour and water which is baked in an oven to make bread.

Emmer
A kind of grain. Like wheat and rye, it is ground into flour and used for making bread.

Festivals
Special days when people worshipped a particular god or goddess. They made sacrifices and held special events in honour of the god.

Hieroglyphics
Egyptian writing. The Ancient Egyptians used pictures for different letters of the alphabet. Each letter is called a hieroglyph.

Incense
A dried gum which comes from certain trees. When it is burnt, it gives off a scented smoke. It was burnt in temples in honour of the gods.

Irrigation
In hot countries water is brought to the fields in narrow ditches from a nearby river.

Mummified
Ancient Egyptians believed that when a person died, his or her soul would need to use the body again. So the body was dried and often pickled before being wrapped in bandages.

Papyrus
Papyrus plants grew at the mouth of the River Nile. The reeds of papyrus plants were used to make paper, ropes, sandals and baskets.

Pestle and mortar
A pestle is a tool used for grinding food or medicines in a bowl called a mortar.

Reservoirs
Containers built out of earth for holding large amounts of water.

Senet
A board game played with counters like draughts or chess.